breakfast

marie claire

breakfast

jody vassallo

marie claire

introduction

The renowned economist J. K. Galbraith once observed, 'it takes some skill to spoil a breakfast,' going on to cheekily add that 'even the English can't do it.' And it's true that in the mornings, we're often happy with the easiest of no-brainer foods — toast, cereal from a box, or poached eggs with grilled tomatoes and bacon, perhaps. Even for those who don't, won't or claim they *can't* cook, breakfast is the simplest of meals to get right; we can all buy jam, slice fresh fruits, spoon out yoghurt and muesli or combine smoothie ingredients in a blender. Sometimes, though, the occasion calls for a little more inspiration — it's easy to fall into a breakfast-time rut. Enter *marie claire Breakfast*! Here you'll find loads of ideas for creating all manner of delicious morning meals; from those in the gratifyingly easy Quick Ideas section, to heartier sweet or savory breakfast options. Chic, snappy and flavorsome, these recipes represent the best of modern cooking. Ingredients are chosen from an international larder (rocket, haloumi, salmon roe, couscous and panettone, for example), flavours are made fresh and zingy by the generous use of herbs, spices and fabulous seasonal produce and the presentation is clean, simple and tantalizing. You'll love the idea of entirely stress-free dishes such as sheep's milk yoghurt served with a swirl of strawberry purée, grilled field mushrooms with garlic and chilli, or that most sexy of fruits, the pomegranate, drizzled with rosewater and apple juice. When friends or family stay for the the night, you can easily turn breakfast the next day into a fun social occasion by whipping up something even more special; corn fritters with crispy prosciutto, maybe, or hearty heuvos rancheros. Poached stone fruits and a batch of passionfruit sugar muffins will hit the sweet spot — although if you feed them this well, your guests may never want to go home! For the traditionalist at heart, too, there's plenty here to satisfy, with livened up versions of breakfast-time classics. You'll find new spins on all the old favorites — a BLT bursts with sunny, Mediterranean flavours (provolone, mortadella and basil), good old chipolatas come with sweet potato and capsicum rosti, and even porridge is elevated to new heights with the addition of cinnamon, caramel and figs.

contents

8   quick ideas

14   savoury

92   sweet

156   index

quick ideas

fresh mixed berries standing alone

chilly iced chocolate

serve toasted panettone with sweet sage,
apple and cinnamon toddies

halved sweet sugar bananas drenched with
golden syrup and finished with chopped
macadamia nuts

espresso with a pinch of ground
cinnamon and cinnamon sticks

sheep's milk yoghurt with puréed
strawberries stirred through

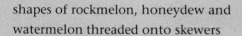

shapes of rockmelon, honeydew and
watermelon threaded onto skewers

fresh passionfruit frozen in their cups

quick ideas

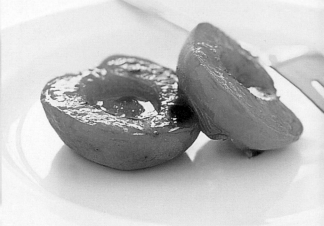

steamed asparagus topped with crispy pancetta and hard-boiled quail eggs

breakfast on grilled apricots and our apricot and bran breakfast shake

colourful fruit platter using mango, guava, grapes, honeydew, kiwi fruit and ripe baby pears

wedges of red papaya drizzled with tangy lime juice

slices of dried fruit, sprinkled with brown sugar and grilled until it caramelizes

sweet fresh figs and fresh dates with thick honey yoghurt sprinkled with toasted pine nuts

pineapple and starfuit slices with maple syrup and shaved toasted coconut

luscious red pomegranates drizzled with combined rosewater and apple juice

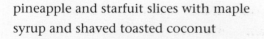

quick ideas

fresh banana and ripe mango blended with vanilla soy and honey yoghurt

chilled fresh guava juice

ginger ale and fresh pineapple juice punch with ginger, strawberries and mint leaves

decadent caffé latte infused with a vanilla bean

cups of ginger tea with lemon grass swizzle sticks

Champagne with strawberries and blackberries

glasses of cardamom caffé latte with a generous nip of frangelico

vodka, tomato juice, a few drops of Tabasco, worcestershire and celery salt

mediterranean blt

4 small vine-ripened tomatoes, halved
1 garlic bulb, halved
1 tablespoon extra virgin olive oil
1 small handful basil leaves
1 loaf crusty bread
8 slices provolone cheese
8 slices mortadella
100 g (3½ oz) rocket (arugula)
extra virgin olive oil, extra, for drizzling
balsamic vinegar, for drizzling

Preheat the oven to 200°C (400°F/Gas 6). Put the tomatoes and garlic in a roasting tin and drizzle with the oil. Sprinkle with sea salt and cracked black pepper and roast for 40 minutes, or until the garlic is soft and the tomatoes are slightly dried. Add the basil leaves and continue cooking for 5 minutes, or until the leaves are crisp. Remove from the oven.

Cut four thick slices from the loaf of crusty bread and lightly toast on both sides. Peel the roasted garlic cloves and spread half onto the toast. Top with the provolone, mortadella, rocket, basil and roasted tomatoes. Sprinkle with the remaining roasted garlic, drizzle with a little extra virgin olive oil and balsamic vinegar and serve immediately.

SERVES 4

salmon, dill and camembert frittata

12 eggs
50 g (1¾ oz/½ cup) grated parmesan cheese
375 ml (13 fl oz/1½ cups) pouring (whipping) cream
6 spring onions (scallions), sliced
200 g (7 oz) smoked salmon
15 g (½ oz/¼ cup) chopped dill
100 g (3½ oz) camembert cheese, sliced
grated zest of 1 lemon
dill sprigs, to garnish

Preheat the oven to 180°C (350°F/Gas 4). Lightly grease and line a 23 cm (9 inch) spring-form cake tin. Lightly beat the eggs, parmesan and cream and stir in the spring onions. Thinly slice 150 g (5½ oz) of the smoked salmon and add it to the egg mixture. Add the dill. Pour the mixture into the tin and place on a baking tray. Bake for 50–60 minutes, or until the frittata has set.

Allow to cool slightly before removing from the tin. Arrange the remaining smoked salmon and all of the sliced camembert decoratively in the centre of the frittata. Sprinkle with lemon zest and serve with dill sprigs.

SERVES 6–8

savoury

fried green tomatoes with haloumi

500 g (1 lb 2 oz) haloumi cheese, cut into 1 cm (½ inch) thick slices
2 garlic cloves, crushed
2 tablespoons lemon juice
1 tablespoon balsamic vinegar
3 tablespoons extra virgin olive oil
250 g (9 oz) cherry tomatoes
250 g (9 oz) teardrop tomatoes, halved
4 green tomatoes, cut into thick slices
125 ml (4 fl oz/½ cup) buttermilk
150 g (5½ oz/1 cup) polenta
oil, for shallow-frying
100 g (3½ oz) rocket (arugula)
2 teaspoons marjoram leaves, to serve

Put the haloumi, garlic, lemon juice, vinegar and olive oil in a non-metallic dish and marinate for at least 3 hours. Drain well and reserve the marinade.

Fry the haloumi in a non-stick frying pan over medium heat until golden brown on both sides. Remove and set aside.

Add the cherry and teardrop tomatoes to the frying pan and cook until the skins burst. Heat the marinade and add to the cooked tomatoes.

Dip the green tomato slices into the buttermilk, then coat in the polenta.

Heat the oil in a large non-stick frying pan and shallow-fry the tomato over medium heat until brown. Drain on paper towel. Serve the haloumi on a bed of rocket topped with tomatoes and drizzled with the reserved marinade. Sprinkle with marjoram leaves.

SERVES 4

sweet potato and capsicum rosti with chipolatas

2 red capsicums (peppers)
500 g (1 lb 2 oz) boiling potatoes, unpeeled
350 g (12 oz) orange sweet potatoes, peeled
1 onion, grated
2 tablespoons chopped coriander (cilantro) leaves
3 tablespoons olive oil
8 chipolatas
100 g (3½ oz) rocket (arugula)
100 g (3½ oz) feta cheese

Grill (broil) the capsicums on high heat until the skins blister. Place in a plastic bag and allow to cool. Peel and cut into strips.

Boil or steam the potatoes and sweet potatoes until tender. Allow to cool slightly, then grate into a bowl. Add the onion, capsicum and coriander.

Heat half of the oil in a large non-stick frying pan, spread the mixture evenly over the base of the pan and cook over medium heat for 10 minutes, or until the base is crisp and golden. Slide the rosti onto a plate, add the remaining oil to the pan, then flip the rosti back into the pan and cook for a further 8 minutes. Remove and keep warm.

Fry the chipolatas until tender, then cut into thick slices. Cut the rosti into wedges and serve topped with rocket, chipolatas and crumbled feta.

SERVES 4–6

corn fritters with crispy prosciutto

8 ripe roma (plum) tomatoes, halved

140 g (5 oz/½ cup) spicy tomato chutney

185 g (6½ oz/1½ cups) self-raising flour

75 g (2½ oz/½ cup) coarse polenta

1 teaspoon sugar

1 egg, lightly beaten

375 ml (13 fl oz/1½ cups) buttermilk

2 corn cobs, kernels removed,
   or 410 g (14½ oz) tinned corn kernels, drained

4 spring onions (scallions), chopped

2 tablespoons snipped chives

25 g (1 oz/¼ cup) grated parmesan cheese

4 tablespoons olive oil

12 thin slices prosciutto

chervil leaves, to serve

Preheat the oven to 200°C (400°F/Gas 6). Place the tomatoes on a non-stick baking tray, sprinkle with salt and pepper and bake for 30 minutes, or until tender. Chop and combine with the chutney.

Sift the flour, polenta and sugar into a large bowl and whisk in the combined egg and buttermilk until smooth. Fold in the corn, spring onions, chives and parmesan. Season with sea salt and freshly ground black pepper.

Heat the oil in a non-stick frying pan and spoon 3 tablespoons of the corn mixture into the pan. Cook for 2 minutes over medium heat. Turn and cook until golden. Repeat with the remaining mixture. Grill (broil) the prosciutto until crisp. Serve the fritters with the tomato chutney, prosciutto and chervil.

SERVES 4

smoky ham, egg and jarlsberg cheese sandwiches

1 unsliced loaf white bread, cut into 2 cm (¾ inch) thick slices
3 tablespoons dijon mustard
1 tablespoon oil
4 eggs
300 g (10½ oz) finely sliced or shaved honey-smoked leg ham
150 g (5½ oz) shaved jarlsberg or Swiss cheese
50 g (1¾ oz) butter, softened

Spread eight slices of bread with the dijon mustard.

Heat the oil in a non-stick frying pan, add the eggs and fry until cooked to your liking (soft in the centre works best). Top four of the slices of bread with some shaved ham, an egg and the cheese, then place the lids on top.

Butter the outside of each sandwich, top and bottom. Heat a frying pan over medium heat and cook the sandwiches in batches, with a plate on top of them to weigh them down, until crisp and golden on both sides. You will know they are ready when the cheese starts melting and oozing out of the sides. Serve immediately.

SERVES 4

NOTE: These sandwiches also work well when made in a toasted sandwich maker.

eggs benedict

HOLLANDAISE SAUCE
175 g (6 oz) butter
4 egg yolks
1 teaspoon tarragon vinegar

4 thick slices rye bread
8 slices of leg ham
1 tablespoon vinegar
8 eggs

To make the hollandaise, melt the butter in a small saucepan. Place the egg yolks, 2 tablespoons water and the tarragon vinegar in a food processor and, with the motor running, gradually add the butter. Process until thick and creamy.

Toast the bread on both sides and top with the sliced ham.

Half-fill a deep frying pan with water, bring to a slow simmer and add the vinegar. One by one, break the eggs onto a plate and slide them into the pan. Cook for 3 minutes, or until done to your liking.

Top each piece of toast and ham with two poached eggs, and drizzle with the hollandaise sauce. Sprinkle with pepper.

SERVES 4

cheese and herb cornbread with scrambled eggs

CORNBREAD
155 g (5½ oz/1¼ cups) self-raising flour
1 tablespoon caster (superfine) sugar
2 teaspoons baking powder
1 teaspoon salt
110 g (3¾ oz/¾ cup) fine polenta
60 g (2¼ oz/½ cup) grated cheddar cheese
1 handful chopped mixed herbs (such as chives, dill, parsley)
2 eggs
250 ml (9 fl oz/1 cup) buttermilk
4 tablespoons macadamia or olive oil

SCRAMBLED EGGS
6 eggs
125 ml (4 fl oz/½ cup) whipping cream
small basil leaves, to garnish

Preheat the oven to 180°C (350°F/Gas 4). Grease a 20 cm x 10 cm (8 inch x 4 inch) loaf (bar) tin. Sift the flour, sugar, baking powder and salt into a bowl. Add the polenta, cheese, herbs, eggs, buttermilk and oil and mix to combine. Spoon the mixture into the loaf tin and bake for 45 minutes, or until a skewer comes out clean when inserted into the cake. Remove from the tin.

To make the scrambled eggs, whisk together the eggs and cream and season. Pour the mixture into a non-stick frying pan and cook over low heat, stirring until the egg is just set. Serve the scrambled eggs with slices of buttered cornbread. Sprinkle with basil leaves.

SERVES 4

savoury

bagels with smoked salmon and caper salsa

4 plain or rye bagels

100 g (3½ oz) neufchatel cream cheese

200 g (7 oz) sliced smoked salmon

2 spring onions (scallions), chopped

2 roma (plum) tomatoes, finely chopped

2 tablespoons baby capers, rinsed and drained

2 tablespoons finely chopped dill

2 tablespoons lemon juice

1 tablespoon extra virgin olive oil

Cut the bagels in half and spread the base generously with cream cheese, then top with the salmon.

Combine the spring onions, tomatoes, capers, dill, lemon juice and olive oil in a bowl. Pile this mixture onto the salmon and serve.

SERVES 4

whitebait with crème fraîche tartare

500 g (1 lb 2 oz) whitebait
125 g (4½ oz/1 cup) plain (all-purpose) flour
vegetable oil, for deep-frying

TARTARE SAUCE
200 g (7 oz) crème fraîche or sour cream
2 tablespoons whole-egg mayonnaise
3 gherkins (pickles), finely chopped
2 tablespoons capers, rinsed, drained and finely chopped
1 teaspoon lemon juice
1 tablespoon chopped flat-leaf (Italian) parsley

Rinse the whitebait and pat dry. Place the flour in a bowl and season with salt and pepper. Toss the whitebait in the flour, shaking off any excess.

Heat the oil in a deep frying pan until a cube of bread browns in 15 seconds when dropped into it. Cook the whitebait, in batches, for 1–2 minutes or until crisp and golden. Remove and drain on paper towels.

To make the tartare sauce, combine the crème fraîche, mayonnaise, gherkins, capers, lemon juice and parsley in a bowl. Serve piles of the fried whitebait on plates, accompanied with a small bowl of tartare sauce.

SERVES 4

crispy lavash tiles with butter mushrooms

3 pieces pitta bread
2 tablespoons olive oil
25 g (1 oz/¼ cup) finely grated parmesan cheese
100 g (3½ oz) butter
4 spring onions (scallions), sliced
750 g (1 lb 10 oz) mixed mushrooms (such as field, button,
    swiss browns, pine, enoki), sliced
1 tablespoon chervil leaves

Preheat the oven to 180°C (350°F/Gas 4). Cut the pitta bread into 3 cm (1¼ inch) wide strips and brush lightly with 1 tablespoon of the oil. Sprinkle with the parmesan cheese and bake for 10 minutes, or until crispy.

Heat the butter and the remaining oil in a large frying pan until sizzling. Add the spring onions and the field mushrooms and cook over medium heat until mushrooms are tender. Add the button mushrooms, swiss browns and pine mushrooms and cook until the liquid has evaporated. Remove from the heat and stir through the enoki mushrooms.

Arrange the toasted strips of bread into an interlocking square. Pile the mushrooms in the centre, top with the chervil and serve immediately.

SERVES 4

individual herbed lemon ricotta

500 g (1 lb 2 oz) ricotta cheese
crusty bread, to serve

DRESSING
2 tablespoons olive oil
1 garlic clove, crushed
zest of 1 lemon
2 tablespoons lemon juice
1 tablespoon balsamic vinegar
125 ml (4 fl oz/½ cup) olive oil
150 g (5½ oz) semi-dried tomatoes, roughly chopped
4 tablespoons chopped flat-leaf (Italian) parsley

Lightly grease and line four 125 ml (4 fl oz/½ cup) ramekins with plastic wrap. Divide the ricotta between the moulds and press down firmly. Cover with plastic wrap and refrigerate for 2 hours.

Preheat the oven to 220°C (425°F/Gas 7). Unmould the ricottas onto a tray lined with baking paper and bake for 20 minutes, or until golden.

To make the dressing, combine all the ingredients in a bowl.

Place each baked ricotta into a shallow bowl and pour a little of the dressing over each one. Serve immediately with crusty bread.

SERVES 4

caramelized leek, goat's cheese and spinach tart

PASTRY
250 g (9 oz) plain (all-purpose) flour
125 g (4½ oz) butter

FILLING
2 tablespoons olive oil
1 leek, thinly sliced
1 head fennel, thinly sliced
150 g (5½ oz) baby English spinach leaves
75 g (2½ oz) goat's cheese, crumbled
3 eggs, lightly beaten
170 ml (5½ fl oz/⅔ cup) pouring (whipping) cream

Preheat the oven to 200°C (400°F/Gas 6). Place the flour and butter in a food processor and process until the mixture resembles breadcrumbs. Gradually add 3–4 tablespoons iced water until the pastry comes together. Gather into a ball, cover with plastic wrap and refrigerate for 20 minutes.

Roll the pastry out on a floured surface to fit a 22 cm (8½ inch) fluted flan tin. Ease into the tin and trim off excess. Line with baking paper and fill with baking weights or rice. Bake for 15 minutes, then remove the weights and paper and bake for 10 minutes. Reduce the oven to 160°C (315°F/Gas 2–3).

Heat the oil in a frying pan over medium heat, add the leek and fennel and cook for 20 minutes. Remove. Add the spinach and cook until wilted. Spread the leek and fennel over the pastry. Top with the spinach and cheese. Combine the eggs and cream, pour into the pastry shell and bake for 40 minutes.

SERVES 6

twice-baked cheese soufflés

250 ml (9 fl oz/1 cup) milk
3 black peppercorns
1 onion, cut in half and studded with 2 cloves
1 bay leaf
60 g (2¼ oz) butter
30 g (1 oz/¼ cup) self-raising flour
2 eggs, separated
125 g (4½ oz) gruyère cheese, grated
250 ml (9 fl oz/1 cup) pouring (whipping) cream
50 g (1¾ oz) parmesan cheese, finely grated

Preheat the oven to 180°C (350°F/Gas 4). Lightly grease four 125 ml (4 fl oz/½-cup) ramekins. Place the milk, peppercorns, onion and bay leaf in a saucepan and heat until almost boiling. Remove from the heat and allow to infuse for 10 minutes. Strain.

Melt the butter in a saucepan, add the flour and cook over medium heat for 1 minute. Remove from the heat and stir in the infused milk, then return to the heat and stir until the mixture thickens. Simmer for 1 minute.

Transfer the mixture to a bowl and add the egg yolks and gruyère cheese. Beat the egg whites until soft peaks form, then gently fold into the cheese sauce. Divide the mixture between the ramekins and place in a baking dish half-filled with hot water. Bake for 15 minutes. Remove from the baking dish, cool and refrigerate. Preheat the oven to 200°C (400°F/Gas 6). Remove the soufflés from the ramekins and place onto ovenproof plates. Pour cream over the top and sprinkle with parmesan. Bake for 20 minutes, or until puffed and golden.

SERVES 4

savoury

potato flowers with salmon, asparagus and quail eggs

DRESSING
60 g (2¼ oz/¼ cup) whole-egg mayonnaise
2 tablespoons plain yoghurt
2 garlic cloves, crushed
1 tablespoon lime juice

125 g (4½ oz) butter
4 potatoes, peeled and cut into paper-thin slices
350 g (12 oz) asparagus spears (24 spears)
8 quail eggs
200 g (7 oz) gravlax slices

Place all the dressing ingredients in a bowl and whisk to combine. Preheat the oven to 240°C (475°F/Gas 9). Melt the butter in a small saucepan. Spoon off any froth that settles on top, and carefully pour off the yellow butter, discarding the milky sediment in the bottom of the pan. Pour half of the butter onto a baking tray. Toss the potato slices in salt, then place four potato slices about 15 cm (6 inches) apart onto the tray. Arrange the remaining slices around them, overlapping to form eight flowers. Brush with a little more butter. Bake for 8 minutes, or until the edges are brown, then turn and cook for a further 3 minutes, or until cooked through. Steam the asparagus spears until tender.

Heat the remaining butter in a non-stick frying pan. Crack the quail eggs using a knife, and cook over low heat for 1–2 minutes or until the whites have set. Serve two potato flowers on each plate, topped with the asparagus, slices of gravlax, two quail eggs and the dressing. Season with pepper.

SERVES 4

mushrooms with marinated feta

20 asparagus spears
300 g (10½ oz) marinated feta cheese
3 tablespoons extra virgin olive oil
zest of 1 lemon
2 garlic cloves, crushed
2 tablespoons lemon juice
4 large field mushrooms, stems removed
2 large tomatoes, cut into thick slices
4 eggs
oregano leaves, to serve

Trim the ends from the asparagus.

Drain the oil from the feta and place into a non-metallic bowl. Stir in the olive oil, lemon zest, garlic and lemon juice. Season with pepper.

Place the mushrooms and tomatoes in a shallow dish and pour the oil mixture over them. Toss gently to coat, and marinate for 15 minutes. Drain the mushrooms, reserving the marinade, and cook, together with the tomatoes, on a lightly oiled barbecue grill plate or flatplate until tender. Add the asparagus towards the end of cooking, and lastly the eggs.

Place the mushrooms on a plate, top each one with some asparagus spears, a slice of tomato, an egg and some sliced feta. Drizzle with the oil marinade and top with oregano.

SERVES 4

squiggly corn crab cakes

100 g (3½ oz) corn spaghetti
500 g (1 lb 2 oz) fresh or tinned crab meat
1 small red capsicum (pepper), finely chopped
1 tablespoon capers, rinsed, drained and roughly chopped
2 tablespoons lime juice
1 teaspoon grated lime zest
1 teaspoon Tabasco sauce
6 spring onions (scallions), chopped
1 egg, lightly beaten
120 g (4¼ oz/1½ cups) fresh breadcrumbs
peanut oil, for shallow-frying
chilli jam, to serve

Cook the pasta in a large saucepan of rapidly boiling water until *al dente*. Drain well and lay out to dry on paper towels, then cut into short lengths.

Combine the pasta, crab, capsicum, capers, lime juice, zest, Tabasco, spring onion, egg and breadcrumbs. Divide the mixture into eight and shape into patties. Place on a tray and refrigerate for 30 minutes.

Heat the oil in a large, deep frying pan to 180°C (350°F), or until a cube of bread browns in 15 seconds when dropped into the oil. Shallow-fry the crab cakes in batches for 3 minutes each side, or until crisp and golden brown. Serve with chilli jam.

SERVES 4

gravlax with parmesan sheets

1 whole salmon, filleted
60 g (2¼ oz) dill, finely chopped
100 g (3½ oz) sea salt
75 g (2½ oz) sugar
1 tablespoon white peppercorns, finely crushed
200 g (7 oz) parmesan cheese, finely grated
sour cream, to serve
chervil, to serve

Place one salmon fillet, skin side down, in a large, shallow, non-metallic dish. Combine the dill, salt, sugar and crushed peppercorns and spread this mixture over the length of the fillet. Place the second salmon fillet on top. Cover with plastic wrap and weigh down with a chopping board and some heavy tins. Refrigerate for two days, turning the salmon as a whole piece every twelve hours and pouring off any excess liquid. When marinated, cut the salmon into wafer-thin slices.

To make the parmesan sheets, preheat the oven to 180°C (350°F/Gas 4). Thinly sprinkle the parmesan in triangle shapes onto two baking trays lined with baking paper. Bake for 10 minutes, or until crisp. Top with gravlax, sour cream, chervil and black pepper.

SERVES 10–12

bruschetta with salmon tartare and roe bubbles

1 loaf crusty bread, cut into 1 cm (½ inch) thick slices
3 garlic cloves, cut in half
extra virgin olive oil, for brushing
500 g (1 lb 2 oz) skinless salmon fillets
2 tablespoons snipped chives
2 tablespoons lime juice
2 tablespoons extra virgin olive oil, extra
100 g (3½ oz) crème fraîche
50 g (1¾ oz) salmon roe

Toast both sides of the bread until golden, then rub one side of each slice with the halved garlic cloves and brush generously with the extra virgin olive oil.

Cut the salmon fillets into 1 cm (½ inch) dice, place in a non-metallic bowl with the chives, lime juice and extra olive oil and season with salt and cracked black pepper. Serve the salmon tartare immediately on the slices of bruschetta, topped with a small spoonful each of crème fraîche and salmon roe.

SERVES 6

rocket, mushroom and blue cheese omelette

40 g (1½ oz) butter
90 g (3¼ oz) field mushrooms, sliced
1 garlic clove, crushed
3 eggs, separated
50 g (1¾ oz) parmesan cheese, finely grated
50 g (1¾ oz) baby rocket (arugula), finely shredded
50 g (1¾ oz) creamy blue cheese, crumbled

Heat 30 g (1 oz) of the butter in a non-stick frying pan. Brown the mushrooms and garlic over high heat for 5 minutes. Remove from the pan.

Whisk the egg whites in a dry bowl until stiff peaks form. Whisk the egg yolks in a separate bowl and season well. Fold the egg whites into the yolks with a large metal spoon, then fold through all but 1 tablespoon of the parmesan along with the mushrooms and rocket.

Heat the remaining butter in the pan until foaming. Pour the egg mixture into the pan and cook over medium heat for 1–2 minutes, or until the omelette starts to come away from the side of the pan.

Sprinkle with the blue cheese and cook under a hot grill (broiler) until just set. Fold the omelette over and slide onto a plate. Top with the reserved parmesan.

SERVES 1

fried haloumi, tomato and rocket sandwiches

500 g (1 lb 2 oz) haloumi cheese, thickly sliced
1 tablespoon finely shredded preserved lemon
2 garlic cloves, crushed
1 tablespoon roughly chopped capers, rinsed and squeezed dry
1 tablespoon extra virgin olive oil
8 thick slices sourdough bread
4 tomatoes, thickly sliced
50 g (1¾ oz) baby rocket (arugula)
50 g (1¾ oz) butter

Put the haloumi in a non-metallic dish. Whisk together the lemon, garlic, capers and olive oil and pour over the haloumi. Toss well, then divide the cheese among four slices of bread. Top with the tomatoes and rocket and season generously. Sandwich with the rest of the bread.

Melt the butter in a large frying pan and cook the sandwiches over medium heat until the bread is crisp and the cheese is soft. Serve immediately.

SERVES 4

scrambled eggs and salmon on croissants

4 eggs
4 tablespoons pouring (whipping) cream
40 g (1½ oz) unsalted butter
125 g (4½ oz) smoked salmon, sliced
2 teaspoons finely chopped dill
2 croissants or 2 individual brioche buns

Beat the eggs and cream together in a bowl. Season with salt and freshly ground black pepper.

Melt the butter in a non-stick frying pan over low heat, then add the eggs. Using a flat-ended wooden spoon, push the mixture around until it starts to set, then add the salmon and dill. Continue to cook, gently folding the salmon and dill through the mixture until the eggs are mostly cooked and there is just a little liquid left in the pan.

Serve the croissants filled with the scrambled eggs.

SERVES 2

savoury breakfast tarts

220 g (7¾ oz/1¾ cups) plain (all-purpose) flour
140 g (5 oz) butter, diced
4 slices ham
2 tablespoons chopped flat-leaf (Italian) parsley
2 tomatoes, finely chopped
8 eggs
125 ml (4 fl oz/½ cup) pouring (whipping) cream
4 tablespoons grated parmesan cheese

Preheat the oven to 200°C (400°F/Gas 6). Sift the flour and ½ teaspoon of salt into a food processor, add the butter and process for a few seconds until the mixture resembles breadcrumbs. Bring the dough together using your hands and shape into a ball. Wrap the ball in plastic wrap, flatten slightly, and put in the fridge for 10 minutes.

Roll the pastry out on a floured work surface until it is very thin. Cut out four 16 cm (6¼ inch) circles and use them to line four 10 cm (4 inch) tartlet tins. Press the pastry gently into the flutes of the tins. Line each tin with a piece of crumpled greaseproof paper and some uncooked rice. Bake the pastry for 10 minutes, then take out the paper and rice and bake for a further minute.

Line each pastry base with the ham (you may need to cut it into pieces to make it fit neatly). Sprinkle with the parsley and add the tomato. Gently break two eggs into each tin, then pour a quarter of the cream over the top of each, sprinkle with parmesan and season with salt and pepper.

Bake the tarts for 15–20 minutes, or until the egg whites are set. Serve hot.

SERVES 4

cheese and onion waffles with herbed ricotta and roast tomato

4 roma (plum) tomatoes, halved
1 tablespoon olive oil
1 tablespoon balsamic vinegar
1 teaspoon sugar
1 tablespoon chopped oregano
310 g (11 oz/1¼ cups) ricotta cheese
4 tablespoons chopped herbs (oregano, sage, rosemary, parsley)
185 g (6½ oz/1½ cups) self-raising flour
3 tablespoons freshly grated parmesan cheese
3 tablespoons grated cheddar cheese
3 large spring onions (scallions), finely chopped
1 egg
250 ml (9 fl oz/1 cup) milk
2 egg whites

Preheat the oven to 160°C (315°F/Gas 2–3). Lightly grease a baking tray. Place the tomato halves on the tray and drizzle with olive oil and balsamic vinegar. Sprinkle with the sugar, oregano and salt. Bake for 1 hour, or until soft.

Put the ricotta in a bowl and fold in the chopped herbs. Season. Divide the herbed ricotta mixture into four even portions. Refrigerate.

Place the flour, parmesan, cheddar, spring onion, whole egg and milk in a bowl. Season, then mix well. Whisk the egg whites, and fold into the cheese and egg mixture. Preheat a waffle iron and brush with olive oil. Pour in 80 ml (2½ fl oz/⅓ cup) waffle batter and cook until golden on both sides. To serve, top the waffles with the tomato halves and ricotta mixture.

SERVES 4

savoury

french toast with crispy prosciutto

3 tablespoons pouring (whipping) cream
3 eggs
3 tablespoons caster (superfine) sugar
pinch of cinnamon
8 thick slices bread, cut in half diagonally
80 g (2¾ oz) butter
1 tablespoon olive oil
12 slices prosciutto
maple syrup, to serve (optional)

Combine the cream, eggs, sugar and cinnamon in a wide, shallow bowl and mix together. Soak the bread in the egg mixture, one slice at a time, shaking off any excess.

Melt half the butter in a frying pan, add 3–4 slices of bread in a single layer and cook until golden brown on both sides. Cook the remaining bread in batches, adding more butter as needed, and keeping the cooked slices warm in the oven.

Heat the olive oil in a frying pan, add the prosciutto and fry until crisp. Remove and drain on paper towels. Place the prosciutto on top of the French toast and serve. Drizzle with maple syrup, if using.

SERVES 4

fried eggs and tomatoes on spring onion potato cakes

300 g (10½ oz) all-purpose potatoes, peeled and roughly chopped
1 egg yolk
50 g (1¾ oz) grated cheddar cheese
3 spring onions (scallions), finely chopped
2 tablespoons finely chopped flat-leaf (Italian) parsley
1 tablespoon plain (all-purpose) flour
4 tablespoons olive oil
1 garlic clove, sliced
3–4 roma (plum) tomatoes, halved lengthways
butter, for frying
4 eggs

Boil the potatoes in a saucepan of salted water until tender. Drain, then mash the potatoes. Stir in the egg yolk, cheese, spring onions and parsley and season. Form into 4 patties. Tip the flour onto a plate and coat the patties with it. Cover and chill for 30 minutes.

Heat 1 tablespoon of the oil in a large frying pan over medium heat. Fry the patties for 4–5 minutes on both sides, or until golden brown. Keep warm.

Heat 1 tablespoon of the oil in the frying pan over low heat. Add the garlic and fry for 2 minutes. Add the tomatoes, cut side down, and fry for 10–15 minutes, turning them once during cooking.

Heat a heavy-based non-stick frying pan over medium heat and add the remaining oil and a little butter. Fry the eggs for about 1 minute. Serve the eggs with the spring onion potato cakes and tomatoes.

SERVES 2–4

grilled field mushrooms with garlic and chilli

40 g (1½ oz) butter, softened
1 garlic clove, crushed
1–2 small red chillies, finely chopped
4 tablespoons finely chopped flat-leaf (Italian) parsley
4 large or 8 medium field mushrooms
4 thick slices ciabatta
tomato chutney or relish, to serve
crème fraîche, to serve

Mix together the butter, garlic, chilli and parsley and spread some over the inside of each mushroom. Season well.

Heat the grill (broiler) to medium and line the base of the grill tray with foil. Grill the mushrooms for about 8 minutes, or until cooked through.

Toast the bread, spread some tomato chutney or relish on each slice, then top with a mushroom (or two) and serve immediately. Serve with a dollop of crème fraîche.

SERVES 4

piperade

2 tablespoons olive oil
1 large onion, thinly sliced
2 red capsicums (peppers), cut into batons
2 garlic cloves, crushed
750 g (1 lb 10 oz) tomatoes
pinch of cayenne pepper
8 eggs, lightly beaten
20 g (¾ oz) butter
4 thin slices ham

Heat the oil in a large heavy-based frying pan over medium heat, then add the onion. Cook for about 3 minutes, or until soft. Add the capsicum and garlic, cover and cook for 8 minutes, stirring frequently.

Score a cross in the base of each tomato. Put in a large bowl of boiling water for 20 seconds, then drain and plunge into a bowl of cold water. Remove the tomatoes and peel the skin away from the cross. Chop the flesh and discard the cores. Add the chopped tomato and cayenne to the capsicum mixture, cover the pan and cook for a further 5 minutes.

Uncover the pan and increase the heat. Cook for 3 minutes, or until the juices have evaporated, shaking the pan often. Season well with salt and freshly ground black pepper.

Add the eggs and scramble into the mixture until fully cooked.

Heat the butter in a small frying pan over medium heat and fry the ham. Arrange the piperade on four plates, top with the cooked ham and serve with buttered toast.

SERVES 4

mushroom omelette with chorizo

50 g (1¾ oz) butter
1 chorizo sausage, sliced
100 g (3½ oz) mushrooms, thinly sliced
6 eggs
2 tablespoons chives, finely chopped

Heat 30 g (1 oz) of the butter in a small omelette pan or frying pan over medium heat. Add the chorizo and fry for about 5 minutes, or until golden. Remove from the pan using a slotted spoon. Add the mushrooms to the pan and cook, stirring frequently, for about 4 minutes, or until soft. Add to the chorizo.

Break the eggs into a bowl and season with salt and freshly ground black pepper. Add the chives and beat lightly with a fork.

Melt half the remaining butter in the pan over medium heat, add half the eggs and cook for 20 seconds, then quickly stir the mixture with a fork. Work quickly, drawing away some of the cooked egg from the bottom of the pan and allowing some of the uncooked egg to set, tilting the pan a little as you go. Once the eggs are mostly set, arrange half the mushrooms and chorizo on top.

Cook for 1 minute more, if necessary. Tip the omelette out onto a plate and keep warm while you cook the second omelette. Serve immediately.

SERVES 2

croque madame

3 eggs
1 tablespoon milk
30 g (1 oz) butter, softened
4 slices white bread
1 teaspoon dijon mustard
4 slices gruyère cheese
2 slices leg ham
2 teaspoons oil

Crack 1 egg into a wide shallow bowl, add the milk and lightly beat. Season with salt and freshly ground black pepper.

Butter the bread using half the butter and spread half the slices with dijon mustard. Place a slice of cheese on top, then the ham and then another slice of cheese. Top with the remaining bread.

Heat the remaining butter and the oil in a large non-stick frying pan over medium heat. While the butter is melting, dip one sandwich into the egg and milk mixture, coating the bread on both sides. When the butter is sizzling, add the sandwich and cook for 1½ minutes on one side, pressing down firmly with a spatula. Turn over and cook the other side, then move it to the side of the pan.

Gently break an egg into the pan and fry until it is done to your liking.

Transfer the sandwich to a plate and top with the fried egg. Keep warm while you repeat with the remaining sandwich and egg, adding more butter and oil to the pan if necessary. Serve immediately.

SERVES 2

huevos rancheros

1½ tablespoons olive oil
1 onion, finely chopped
1 green capsicum (pepper), finely chopped
2 red chillies, finely chopped
1 garlic clove, crushed
½ teaspoon dried oregano
2 tomatoes, chopped
800 g (1 lb 12 oz) tinned chopped tomatoes
8 eggs
4 flour tortillas
100 g (3½ oz/⅔ cup) crumbled feta cheese

Heat the olive oil in a large frying pan over medium heat. Add the onion and green capsicum and fry for 3 minutes, or until soft.

Add the chilli and garlic and stir, then add the oregano, fresh and tinned tomatoes, and 185 ml (6 fl oz/¾ cup) water. Bring to the boil, then reduce the heat, cover with a lid and simmer gently for 8–10 minutes, or until the sauce thickens. Season with salt and pepper.

Smooth the surface of the mixture, then make eight hollows with the back of a spoon. Break an egg into each hollow and put the lid on the pan. Cook the eggs for 5 minutes, or until they are set.

While the eggs are cooking, heat the tortillas according to the instructions on the packet and cut each into quarters.

Serve the eggs with some feta crumbled over them and the tortillas on the side.

SERVES 2

spanish omelette with smoked salmon

1 tablespoon olive oil
400 g (14 oz) all-purpose potatoes, peeled and cubed
1 onion, finely chopped
8 eggs
2 tablespoons chopped dill
8 slices smoked salmon
80 g (2¾ oz/⅓ cup) mascarpone cheese
4 handfuls salad leaves

Heat the oil in a non-stick frying pan and add the potato. Fry gently, stirring, for 10 minutes, or until browned on all sides and cooked through.

Add the onion to the pan and cook for 2–3 minutes, or until translucent and soft. Heat the grill (broiler) to medium.

Whisk the eggs in a bowl together with the dill and some salt and freshly ground black pepper.

Tear the smoked salmon into pieces and add to the frying pan. Add the mascarpone in dollops. Using a spatula, pull the mixture into the centre of the pan and level it off.

Pour the eggs over the top and cook for 5–10 minutes, or until the omelette is just set.

Put the frying pan under the grill for 1–2 minutes to lightly brown the top. Slide the omelette out of the frying pan and cut into eight wedges. Arrange a handful of salad leaves on each plate and top with two wedges of omelette.

SERVES 4

savoury

fried egg and red onion wrap

1½ tablespoons olive oil
3 red onions, thickly sliced
1 large red capsicum (pepper), sliced
3 tablespoons balsamic vinegar
4 eggs
4 pieces lavash or other unleavened bread
4 tablespoons sour cream
sweet chilli sauce, to serve

Heat the olive oil in a non-stick frying pan over medium heat and add the onion. Cook, stirring occasionally, until soft and translucent. Add the red capsicum and cook until soft. Increase the heat and stir for 1–2 minutes, or until they start to brown, then stir in the balsamic vinegar. Remove the mixture from the pan and keep warm.

Carefully break the eggs into the frying pan and, keeping them separate, cook over low heat until they are just set.

Heat the lavash bread under a grill (broiler) for a few seconds. Spread 1 tablespoon of sour cream onto the centre of each piece of bread, then drizzle with some of the sweet chilli sauce. Top with the onion and capsicum mixture and an egg. Season with salt and pepper.

Fold in one short end of each piece of lavash bread and then roll up each one lengthways.

SERVES 4

salmon and dill potato patties with lime mayonnaise

400 g (14 oz) new potatoes, cut in half
2 teaspoons grated lime zest
310 g (11 oz/1¼ cups) whole-egg mayonnaise
425 g (15 oz) tinned salmon, drained, bones removed
1 tablespoon chopped dill
2 spring onions (scallions), thinly sliced
1 egg
80 g (2¾ oz/1 cup) fresh breadcrumbs
3 tablespoons oil
200 g (7 oz) rocket (arugula)
lime wedges, to serve

Cook the potatoes in a large saucepan of boiling water for 12–15 minutes, or until tender. Drain well and cool.

Combine the lime zest and 250 g (9 oz/1 cup) of the mayonnaise.

Transfer the potato to a large bowl, then mash roughly with the back of a spoon, leaving some large chunks. Stir in the salmon, dill and spring onion and season. Mix in the egg and the remaining mayonnaise. Divide into eight portions, forming palm-size patties. Press lightly into the breadcrumbs to coat.

Heat the oil in a non-stick frying pan over medium heat and cook the patties, turning, for 3–4 minutes, or until golden brown. Drain on paper towels. Serve with a dollop of lime mayonnaise, rocket leaves and lime wedges.

SERVES 4

savoury

classic omelette

12 eggs
40 g (1½ oz) butter

Beat the eggs in a bowl together with 160 ml (5¼ fl oz) water and season with salt and freshly ground black pepper.

Heat 10 g (¼ oz) of the butter in a small frying pan or omelette pan over high heat. When the butter is foaming, reduce the heat to medium and add one-quarter of the egg mixture. Tilt the pan to cover the base with the egg and leave for a few seconds. Using a spatula, draw the sides of the omelette into the centre and let any extra liquid egg run to the edges.

If you are adding a filling to the omelette, sprinkle it over the egg. As soon as the egg is almost set, use an egg slide to fold the omelette in half in the pan. It should still be soft inside. Slide it onto a warm serving plate and repeat to make 3 more omelettes.

SERVES 4

FILLINGS: Sprinkle each omelette with 15 g (½ oz/⅓ cup) roughly torn rocket (arugula) and 50 g (1¾ oz) crumbled goat's cheese.

Sauté 250 g (9 oz) finely sliced button mushrooms in 50 g (1¾ oz) butter, add 4 tablespoons finely chopped basil.

herbed garlic mushrooms with goat's cheese bruschetta

80 g (2¾ oz) butter
4 garlic cloves, crushed
20 g (¾ oz) chopped flat-leaf (Italian) parsley
4 large field mushrooms, stalks removed
4 large slices crusty bread
2 tablespoons olive oil
150 g (5½ oz) goat's cheese, at room temperature
40 g (1½ oz) baby rocket (arugula)

Preheat the oven to 180°C (350°F/Gas 4). Melt the butter in a small saucepan, add the garlic and parsley and cook, stirring, for 1 minute, or until well combined. Spoon the mixture evenly over the underside of the mushrooms. Line a baking tray with baking paper. Place the mushrooms on the tray, filling side up, and cover with foil. Bake for 20 minutes, or until softened and cooked through.

Brush both sides of the bread with the olive oil and grill (broil) until crisp and golden on both sides.

Spread the bruschetta with the soft goat's cheese and top with the rocket. Cut the garlic mushrooms in half and place two halves on each bruschetta, then drizzle with the cooking juices and season with ground black pepper. Serve immediately.

SERVES 4

mini sweet potato and leek frittatas

500 g (1 lb 2 oz) orange sweet potato
1 tablespoon olive oil
15 g (½ oz) butter
2 leeks, white part only, thinly sliced
1 garlic clove, crushed
125 g (4½ oz) feta cheese, crumbled
8 eggs
125 ml (4 fl oz/½ cup) pouring (whipping) cream
rocket (arugula), to serve (optional)

Preheat the oven to 180°C (350°F/Gas 4). Grease twelve regular muffin holes. Cut small rounds of baking paper and place into the base of each hole. Cut the sweet potato into small cubes and steam until tender. Drain well and set aside.

Heat the oil and butter in a large frying pan, add the leek and cook for 10 minutes, stirring occasionally, or until very soft and lightly golden. Add the garlic and cook for a further 1 minute. Cool, then stir in the feta and sweet potato. Divide the mixture evenly among the muffin holes.

Whisk the eggs and cream together and season with salt and freshly ground black pepper. Pour the egg mixture into each hole until three-quarters filled, then press the vegetables down gently. Bake for 25–30 minutes, or until golden and set. Leave in the tins for 5 minutes, then ease out with a knife and cool on a wire rack before serving. Serve with rocket.

MAKES 12 FRITTATAS

potato tortilla

500 g (1 lb 2 oz) potatoes, cut into 1 cm (½ inch) slices
3 tablespoons olive oil
1 onion, thinly sliced
4 garlic cloves, thinly sliced
2 tablespoons finely chopped flat-leaf (Italian) parsley
6 eggs

Place the potato slices in a large saucepan, cover with cold water and bring to the boil over high heat. Boil for 5 minutes, then drain and set aside.

Heat the oil in a deep-sided non-stick frying pan over medium heat. Add the onion and garlic and cook for 5 minutes, or until the onion softens.

Add the potato and parsley to the pan and stir to combine. Cook over medium heat for 5 minutes, gently pressing down into the pan.

Whisk the eggs with 1 teaspoon each of salt and freshly ground black pepper and pour evenly over the potato. Cover and cook over medium heat for about 20 minutes, or until the egg is just set. Cut into wedges to serve.

SERVES 6–8

savoury

kedgeree

350 g (12 oz) undyed smoked haddock
3 slices lemon
1 bay leaf
300 ml (10½ fl oz) milk
175 g (6 oz) long-grain rice
60 g (2¼ oz) butter
1 small onion, finely chopped
2 teaspoons mild curry powder
1 tablespoon finely chopped flat-leaf (Italian) parsley
3 eggs, hard-boiled, roughly chopped
170 ml (5½ fl oz/⅔ cup) thick (double/heavy) cream
mango chutney, to serve

Put the smoked haddock in a deep frying pan with the lemon and bay leaf, cover with the milk and simmer for 6 minutes, or until cooked through. Remove the fish and break into large flakes. Discard any bones.

Put the rice in a saucepan along with 350 ml (12 fl oz) water, bring to the boil, cover and cook for 10 minutes, or until just cooked. Drain any excess water and fork through to fluff up the rice.

Melt the butter in a frying pan over medium heat. Add the onion and cook for 3 minutes, or until soft. Add the curry powder and cook for a further 2 minutes. Add the rice and stir through, cooking for 2–3 minutes, or until heated through. Add the fish, parsley, egg and cream and stir until heated through. Season with pepper. Serve with mango chutney.

SERVES 4

apricot and bran breakfast shake

100 g (3½ oz) dried apricots
1 tablespoon oat bran
1 tablespoon honey
3 tablespoons apricot yoghurt
600 ml (21 fl oz) milk

Pour enough boiling water over the dried apricots to cover them, then leave until they are plump and rehydrated. Drain well.

Place the apricots, oat bran, honey, yoghurt and milk in a blender and mix until thick and smooth. Divide among glasses to serve.

SERVES 2–4

creamy rich banana and macadamia smoothie

2 bananas, slightly frozen
100 g (3½ oz) honey-roasted macadamia nuts
2 tablespoons vanilla and honey yoghurt
2 tablespoons wheat germ
500 ml (17 fl oz/2 cups) milk
1 banana, extra, cut in half lengthways

Place the frozen bananas, 60 g (2¼ oz) of the macadamia nuts, the yoghurt, wheat germ and milk in a blender and whizz for several minutes until thick and creamy.

Finely chop the remaining macadamias and put on a plate. Toss the banana halves in the nuts to coat.

Stand a banana half in each glass and then pour in the smoothie.

SERVES 2

pandoro with poached peaches and mascarpone

220 g (7¾ oz/1 cup) sugar
3 cardamom pods, bruised
1 bay leaf
1 vanilla bean, split
juice of 1 lemon
6 freestone peaches
4 baby pandoro, cut into thick slices, or 1 baby panettone, sliced
2 eggs, lightly beaten
500 ml (17 fl oz/2 cups) milk
50 g (1¾ oz) butter
200 g (7 oz) mascarpone cheese or sour cream
3 tablespoons soft brown sugar
bay leaves, to garnish

Place the sugar, 1 litre (35 fl oz/4 cups) water, cardamom pods, bay leaf, vanilla bean and lemon juice into a large saucepan and stir over low heat until the sugar dissolves. Bring to the boil and add the peaches. Reduce the heat and simmer for 10 minutes. Remove the peaches, peel and halve. Boil the syrup until reduced by a third.

Dip the pandoro or panettone into the combined egg and milk mixture. Heat the butter in a large frying pan and cook the pandoro or panettone in batches over medium heat until golden brown on both sides.

Combine the mascarpone and brown sugar. Arrange the pandoro or panettone slices on plates, top with the mascarpone mixture and peaches and drizzle with the syrup. Garnish with a bay leaf.

SERVES 4

sweet

maple yoghurt balls with sugary balsamic pears

1 kg (2 lb 4 oz) Greek-style yoghurt
125 ml (4 fl oz/½ cup) maple syrup
square of muslin (cheesecloth)
1 tablespoon ground cinnamon
2 tablespoons caster (superfine) sugar
200 g (7 oz) hazelnuts, toasted and roughly chopped
150 g (5½ oz) butter
95 g (3¼ oz/½ cup) soft brown sugar
3 tablespoons balsamic vinegar
3 small beurre bosc pears, sliced lengthways

Combine the yoghurt and maple syrup, place onto a large square of doubled muslin, gather the muslin together and tie tightly together with string. Loop the string around a chopstick and suspend over a bowl in the refrigerator for 4 days to remove any liquid.

Form 1 tablespoon of the mixture into a ball with moistened hands and roll in the combined cinnamon and caster sugar mixture. Then toss to coat in the chopped hazelnuts. Repeat with the remaining mixture.

Heat the butter in a large frying pan, add the brown sugar and stir over low heat until it dissolves. Stir in the balsamic vinegar and bring the mixture to the boil. Add the pears and simmer until browned on both sides and slightly soft. Arrange on serving plates and top with the yoghurt balls.

SERVES 4

healthy nut and seed muesli

100 g (3½ oz) puffed corn
150 g (5½ oz) rolled oats
100 g (3½ oz/1 cup) pecans
160 g (5¾ oz/1 cup) macadamia nuts, roughly chopped
100 g (3½ oz) flaked coconut
200 g (7 oz) LSA (linseed, sunflower and almond) mix
100 g (3½ oz) dried apples, chopped
200 g (7 oz) dried apricots, chopped
125 g (4½ oz) dried pears, chopped
125 ml (4 fl oz/½ cup) maple syrup
1 teaspoon natural vanilla extract

Preheat the oven to 180°C (350°F/Gas 4). Place the puffed corn, rolled oats, pecans, macadamia nuts, coconut, LSA mix, apples, apricots and pears in a bowl and mix to combine.

Place the maple syrup and vanilla in a small saucepan and cook over low heat for 3 minutes or until the maple syrup becomes easy to pour.

Pour the maple syrup over the nut mixture and toss lightly to coat.

Divide the muesli mixture between two non-stick baking dishes. Bake for about 20 minutes, turning frequently, until the muesli is lightly toasted. Allow the mixture to cool before transferring it to an airtight container.

MAKES 1 KG (2 LB 4 OZ)

cinnamon porridge with caramel figs and cream

200 g (7 oz/2 cups) rolled oats
1/4 teaspoon ground cinnamon
50 g (1 3/4 oz) butter
95 g (3 1/4 oz/1/2 cup) soft brown sugar
300 ml (10 1/2 fl oz) pouring (whipping) cream
6 figs, halved
milk, to serve
100 g (3 1/2 oz) thick (double/heavy) cream, to serve

Place the oats, 1 litre (35 fl oz/4 cups) water and cinnamon in a saucepan and stir over medium heat for 5 minutes, or until the porridge becomes thick and smooth. Set the porridge aside.

Melt the butter in a large frying pan, add all but 2 tablespoons of the brown sugar and stir until it dissolves. Stir in the cream and bring to the boil, then simmer for 5 minutes or until the sauce starts to thicken slightly.

Place the figs onto a baking tray, sprinkle with the remaining sugar and grill (broil) until the sugar is melted.

Spoon the porridge into individual bowls and top with a little milk, then divide the figs and the caramel sauce among the bowls. Top each serving with a large dollop of thick cream.

SERVES 4

mixed berry couscous

185 g (6½ oz/1 cup) couscous
500 ml (17 fl oz/2 cups) apple and cranberry juice
1 cinnamon stick
150 g (5½ oz) raspberries
150 g (5½ oz) blueberries
150 g (5½ oz) blackberries
150 g (5½ oz) strawberries, halved
zest of 1 lime
zest of 1 orange
200 g (7 oz) Greek-style yoghurt
2 tablespoons golden or maple syrup
mint leaves, to garnish

Place the couscous in a bowl.

Place the apple and cranberry juice in a saucepan with the cinnamon stick. Bring to the boil, then remove from the heat and pour over the couscous. Cover with plastic wrap and allow to stand for 5 minutes, or until all the liquid has been absorbed. Remove and discard the cinnamon stick.

Separate the grains of the couscous with a fork, add the raspberries, blueberries, blackberries, strawberries, lime zest and orange zest and fold through gently. Spoon the mixture into four bowls and serve with a generous dollop of yoghurt and a drizzle of golden or maple syrup. Garnish with mint leaves.

SERVES 4

sweet

ginger and ricotta hotcakes with fresh honeycomb

150 g (5½ oz/1 cup) wholemeal plain (all-purpose) flour
2 teaspoons baking powder
2 teaspoons ground ginger
2 tablespoons caster (superfine) sugar
55 g (2 oz/1 cup) flaked coconut, toasted
4 eggs, separated
500 g (1 lb 2 oz) ricotta cheese
310 ml (10¾ fl oz/1¼ cups) milk
4 bananas, sliced
200 g (7 oz) fresh honeycomb, broken into large pieces

Sift the flour, baking powder, ginger and sugar into a bowl. Stir in the coconut and make a well in the centre. Add the combined egg yolks, 350 g (12 oz) of the ricotta and all of the milk. Mix until smooth.

Beat the egg whites until soft peaks form, then gently fold into the hotcake mixture.

Heat a frying pan and brush lightly with a little melted butter or oil. Pour 3 tablespoons of the batter into the pan and swirl gently to create an even hotcake. Cook over low heat until bubbles form on the surface. Flip and cook the other side for 1 minute, or until golden. Continue until all the batter is used up.

Stack three hotcakes onto each plate and top with a generous dollop of ricotta, sliced banana and a large piece of fresh honeycomb.

SERVES 4

choc-hazelnut puff pastry rolls

80 g (2¾ oz) choc-hazelnut spread
80 g (2¾ oz) icing (confectioners') sugar
2 sheets puff pastry, thawed
1 egg, lightly beaten
icing (confectioners') sugar, for dusting

Preheat the oven to 200°C (400°F/Gas 6). Combine the choc-hazelnut spread and icing sugar and roll into a 20 cm (8 inch) long roll. Wrap the roll in plastic wrap and twist the ends to enclose. Refrigerate for 30 minutes. When firm, cut the roll into eight even pieces. Roll each of the pieces in icing sugar.

Cut each sheet of puff pastry into four squares. Place a piece of the choc-hazelnut roll onto each square of pastry and roll up to enclose. Pinch the ends and brush lightly with egg. Bake for 15 minutes, or until the pastry is golden. Dust with icing sugar.

SERVES 4

pecan filo sheets with fried apples

8 sheets filo pastry
50 g (1¾ oz) butter, melted
125 g (4½ oz) pecans, chopped
45 g (1½ oz/¼ cup) soft brown sugar
80 g (2¾ oz) butter, extra
½ teaspoon freshly grated nutmeg
1 teaspoon ground cinnamon
¼ teaspoon ground cloves
4 small granny smith apples, sliced into 1 cm
    (½ inch) thick slices horizontally (do not peel or core)
200 g (7 oz) fromage frais
extra nutmeg, for dusting

Preheat the oven to 200°C (400°F/Gas 6). Brush one sheet of filo pastry with the melted butter. Top with another sheet, sprinkle with one-third of the pecans and sugar, top with another layer of filo, brush with butter and repeat the layering and sprinkling until you have used all the pastry, pecans and sugar. Use scissors to cut the pastry in half, then cut each half into eight triangles. Place the triangles on two baking trays and bake for 10 minutes, or until crisp and golden.

Heat the extra butter in a large frying pan, add the spices and apples and cook over medium heat for 5 minutes, turning the apples once, until they are soft and golden. Serve accompanied with filo triangles and a spoonful of fromage frais. Dust with nutmeg.

SERVES 4–6

star anise, lime and vanilla tropical fruit salad

1 kg (2 lb 4 oz) watermelon, cut into large pieces
1 small pineapple, chopped
2 mangoes, sliced
1 guava, sliced
1 small red papaya, cut into large pieces
12 lychees, peeled
3 kiwi fruit, sliced
3 tablespoons lime juice
100 g (3½ oz/¾ cup) grated light palm sugar (jaggery) or
    soft brown sugar
6 star anise
1 vanilla bean, split in half
1 pandanus leaf, knotted
zest of 1 lime

Place the watermelon, pineapple, mangoes, guava, papaya, lychees and kiwi fruit in a bowl and gently combine.

Place the lime juice, palm sugar, star anise, vanilla bean, pandanus leaf, lime zest and 250 ml (9 fl oz/1 cup) water in a saucepan and stir over low heat until the sugar dissolves. Bring to the boil, reduce the heat and simmer for 10 minutes or until the syrup is reduced by half. Allow to cool slightly.

Pour the syrup over the fruit and refrigerate until cold.

SERVES 6

pancakes with rosewater strawberries and butter

185 g (6½ oz/1½ cups) self-raising flour
2 tablespoons caster (superfine) sugar
2 eggs, lightly beaten
250 ml (9 fl oz/1 cup) milk
60 g (2¼ oz) butter, melted, plus extra
230 g (8½ oz/1 cup) caster (superfine) sugar, extra
1 tablespoon ground cinnamon
400 g (14 oz) strawberries, halved
2 teaspoons rosewater
1 teaspoon natural vanilla extract
3 tablespoons maple syrup
100 g (3½ oz) butter, softened and whipped

Sift the flour, sugar and a pinch of salt into a bowl and make a well in the centre. Mix together the eggs, milk and butter in a jug and pour into the well. Whisk to form a smooth batter. Cover and allow to stand for 20 minutes.

Heat a non-stick frying pan and brush with extra melted butter. Add 3 tablespoons of batter into the pan and swirl gently. Cook over low heat for 1 minute, or until bubbles burst on the surface. Turn the pancake over and cook the other side. Transfer to a plate and keep warm while cooking the remaining batter.

Combine the extra sugar and cinnamon and toss each pancake in the mixture. Combine the strawberries, rosewater, vanilla and maple syrup. Serve stacks of the pancakes topped with whipped butter and the strawberry mixture.

SERVES 4

high-top cappuccino and white-choc muffins

20 g (¾ oz/¼ cup) instant espresso coffee powder
310 g (11 oz/2½ cups) self-raising flour
115 g (4 oz/½ cup) caster (superfine) sugar
2 eggs, lightly beaten
375 ml (13 fl oz/1½ cups) buttermilk
1 teaspoon natural vanilla extract
150 g (5½ oz) butter, melted
100 g (3½ oz) white chocolate, roughly chopped
30 g (1 oz) butter, extra
3 tablespoons soft brown sugar

Preheat the oven to 200°C (400°F/Gas 6). Cut eight lengths of baking paper and roll into 8 cm (3 inch) high cylinders to fit into eight 125 ml (4 fl oz/ ½ cup) capacity ramekins. When in place in the ramekins, secure the cylinders with string and place all the ramekins onto a baking tray.

Dissolve the coffee in 1 tablespoon of boiling water and allow to cool. Sift the flour and caster sugar into a bowl. Combine the eggs, buttermilk, vanilla, melted butter, white chocolate and the coffee mixture and mix roughly with the dry ingredients. Spoon the mixture into each cylinder. Heat the extra butter and brown sugar and stir until the sugar dissolves. Spoon this mixture onto each muffin and gently swirl into the muffin using a skewer. Bake for 25–30 minutes, or until risen and cooked when tested with a skewer.

MAKES 8 MUFFINS

raspberry marshmallow friands

125 g (4½ oz/1 cup) plain (all-purpose) flour
185 g (6½ oz/1½ cups) icing (confectioners') sugar
100 g (3½ oz) ground hazelnuts
45 g (1½ oz/½ cup) desiccated coconut
5 egg whites
180 g (6½ oz) butter, melted and cooled
100 g (3½ oz) raspberries
50 g (1¾ oz) small pink marshmallows, chopped
10 small pink marshmallows, extra

Preheat the oven to 200°C (400°F/Gas 6). Lightly grease 10 friand tins.

Sift the flour and icing sugar into a bowl. Stir in the ground hazelnuts and coconut.

Whisk the egg whites in a clean, dry bowl until foamy. Fold into the dry ingredients with the melted butter.

Set aside 20 of the raspberries, then carefully fold the rest into the mixture with the chopped marshmallows. Spoon into the tins. Press a halved marshmallow and two raspberries into the top of each friand.

Bake for 20 minutes, or until golden and starting to come away from the sides of the tins. Leave to cool for 5 minutes in the tins before turning out onto a wire rack to cool completely.

MAKES 10 FRIANDS

rhubarb with vanilla and cardamom rice

1 litre (35 fl oz/4 cups) milk
220 g (7¾ oz/1 cup) sugar
1 vanilla bean, split in half and seeds scraped out
4 cardamom pods, bruised
220 g (7¾ oz/1 cup) arborio rice
200 g (7 oz) mascarpone cheese (optional)
500 g (1 lb 2 oz) rhubarb, cut into short lengths
95 g (3¼ oz/½ cup) soft brown sugar
1 cinnamon stick

Put the milk, sugar, vanilla bean and cardamom in a saucepan and heat until just about to boil. Add the rice and cook, stirring, for 20–30 minutes, or until tender.

Add the mascarpone, if using, and beat until thick and creamy. Remove the vanilla bean and cardamom.

Put the rhubarb, brown sugar, cinnamon and 3 tablespoons water in a saucepan, cover with a tight-fitting lid and cook over medium heat for 5 minutes. Stir and check to see how soft the rhubarb is. It should break into strands. If it doesn't, cook for a few more minutes, taking care not to overcook or it will become mushy. Serve with the creamed rice.

SERVES 4

banana, sunflower and pistachio bread

100 g (3½ oz) butter, softened
120 g (4 oz/¾ cup) muscovado sugar
2 eggs, lightly beaten
500 g (1 lb 2 oz) ripe bananas, mashed
100 g (3½ oz) shelled pistachio nuts, roughly chopped
60 g (2¼ oz/½ cup) sunflower seeds
250 g (9 oz/2 cups) self-raising flour
1 teaspoon bicarbonate of soda (baking soda)
½ teaspoon mixed spice
honey, to serve

Preheat the oven to 180°C (350°F/Gas 4). Grease and line the base of a 23 cm (9 inch) loaf (bar) tin.

Beat the butter and sugar until light and creamy. Add the eggs gradually, beating well after each addition. Stir in the bananas, nuts and seeds.

Sift together the flour, bicarbonate of soda and mixed spice, then fold into the banana mixture.

Spoon into the tin and bake for 1 hour, or until a skewer comes out clean when inserted into the centre. Leave to cool in the tin for 15 minutes before turning out onto a wire rack to cool completely. Serve buttered and drizzled with runny honey.

SERVES 6–8

passionfruit sugar muffins

310 g (11 oz/2½ cups) self-raising flour
350 g (12 oz/1½ cups) caster (superfine) sugar
375 ml (13 fl oz/1½ cups) buttermilk
2 eggs
1 teaspoon natural vanilla extract
250 g (9 oz) butter, melted and cooled
60 g (2¼ oz/¼ cup) passionfruit curd
1–2 tablespoons lemon juice

Preheat the oven to 190°C (375°F/Gas 5). Lightly grease 12 regular muffin holes. Sift the flour into a bowl and stir in 115 g (4 oz/½ cup) of the caster sugar. Make a well in the centre.

Whisk together the buttermilk, eggs, vanilla and 150 g (5½ oz) of the melted butter and pour into the well. Stir until only just combined (the mixture should still be lumpy).

Half-fill each muffin hole with mixture, then add 1 teaspoon of passionfruit curd to each muffin and top up with the remaining mixture. Bake for 30 minutes, or until risen and springy to touch.

Mix the lemon juice and remaining butter in a bowl and spread the remaining sugar on a plate. Brush the warm muffins with lemon butter and roll in the sugar. Repeat and serve warm.

MAKES 12 MUFFINS

sweet

brioche eggy bread with figs and raspberry cream

4 small brioche
3 eggs, lightly beaten
250 ml (9 fl oz/1 cup) milk
1 teaspoon almond extract
50 g (1¾ oz) butter
6 figs, quartered
2 tablespoons soft brown sugar

RASPBERRY CREAM
200 g (7 oz) raspberries
200 g (7 oz) sour cream
3 tablespoons soft brown sugar

Cut the brioche lengthways into thick slices. Whisk together the eggs, milk and almond extract.

Heat half the butter in a large frying pan. Dip a slice of brioche in the egg mixture, letting any extra drain off, then lay in the pan. Fry over medium heat until golden brown on both sides. Keep warm while you cook the rest, adding more butter to the pan as you need it.

Arrange the figs, cut side up, on a baking tray, sprinkle lightly with the sugar and grill (broil) until the sugar has caramelized and the figs have softened.

To make the raspberry cream, lightly crush the raspberries with a fork. Stir through the sour cream with the brown sugar. Serve with the brioche and figs.

SERVES 4

poached stone fruits

230 g (8½ oz/1 cup) caster (superfine) sugar
1 cinnamon stick
3 star anise
6 cloves
500 g (1 lb 2 oz) apricots
1 kg (2 lb 4 oz) freestone peaches
500 g (1 lb 2 oz) nectarines

Put the sugar, cinnamon, star anise and cloves in a saucepan with 1 litre (35 fl oz/4 cups) water and stir over low heat until the sugar has dissolved.

Bring to the boil, add the fruit and simmer for 10 minutes or until soft. Remove the fruit, peel and halve.

Simmer the liquid for 10 minutes, or until thickened slightly.

Place the fruit in a bowl, pour the syrup over the top and leave to cool. Store in a vacuum-sealed glass jar in the fridge for up to 3 weeks.

Serve with thick yoghurt or on top of breakfast cereals.

SERVES 6–8

creamed rice with minted citrus compote

150 g (5½ oz/¾ cup) basmati rice
500 ml (17 fl oz/2 cups) milk
4 cardamom pods, bruised
½ cinnamon stick
1 clove
3 tablespoons honey
1 teaspoon natural vanilla extract

MINTED CITRUS COMPOTE
2 pink grapefruit, segmented
2 oranges, segmented
3 tablespoons orange juice
1 teaspoon grated lime zest
3 tablespoons honey
8 mint leaves, finely chopped

Cook the rice in a large saucepan of boiling water for 12 minutes, stirring occasionally. Drain and cool.

Place the rice, milk, cardamom pods, cinnamon stick and clove in a saucepan and bring to the boil. Reduce the heat to low and simmer for 15 minutes, stirring occasionally, until the milk is absorbed and the rice is creamy. Remove the spices, then stir in the honey and vanilla.

To make the compote, combine the pink grapefruit, orange, orange juice, lime zest, honey and mint and mix until the honey has dissolved. Serve with the rice.

SERVES 4

blueberry pancakes

250 ml (9 fl oz/1 cup) buttermilk
1 egg, lightly beaten
20 g (¾ oz) butter, melted
1 teaspoon natural vanilla extract
90 g (3¼ oz/¾ cup) plain (all-purpose) flour
1 teaspoon baking powder
2 ripe bananas, mashed
100 g (3½ oz) blueberries, plus extra, to serve
1 teaspoon oil
maple syrup, to serve

Put the buttermilk, egg, butter and vanilla extract in a bowl and whisk together. Sift in the flour, baking powder and ½ teaspoon salt, then stir, making sure not to overblend as the batter should be lumpy. Add the fruit.

Heat the oil in a frying pan over medium heat. Add 2 tablespoons of batter to the pan for each pancake. Cook for 3 minutes, or until the pancakes are golden brown on the bottom. Turn over and cook for a further 1 minute. Repeat with the rest of the batter, keeping the cooked pancakes warm. Serve immediately, with extra blueberries and maple syrup.

MAKES ABOUT 12 PANCAKES

grilled nectarines with cinnamon toast

40 g (1½ oz) low-fat margarine
1 teaspoon ground cinnamon
4 thick slices brioche
6 ripe nectarines, halved and stones removed
icing (confectioners') sugar, to serve
2 tablespoons warmed blossom honey

Place the margarine and cinnamon in a bowl and mix until well combined. Grill (broil) the brioche on one side until golden. Spread the other side with half the cinnamon spread, then grill until golden. Keep warm in the oven.

Brush the nectarines with the remaining spread and cook under a grill (broiler) or on a ridged grill plate, until the spread is bubbling and the fruit is tinged at the edges.

To serve, place 3 nectarine halves on each toasted slice of brioche. Dust with the icing sugar and drizzle with the warmed honey.

SERVES 4

NOTE: Tinned plums or apricots may be used in place of nectarines.

raspberry breakfast crepes

250 g (9 oz/2 cups) plain (all-purpose) flour
1 teaspoon sugar
2 eggs, lightly beaten
500 ml (17 fl oz/2 cups) milk
20 g (¾ oz) butter, melted
400 g (14 oz/3⅓ cups) raspberries
icing (confectioners') sugar, for dusting
maple syrup or honey, to serve

Sift the flour, sugar and a pinch of salt into a bowl and make a well in the centre. In a bowl, mix the eggs and milk together with 100 ml (3½ fl oz) water. Slowly pour the mixture into the well, whisking all the time to incorporate the flour and ensure a smooth batter. Stir in the melted butter. Cover and refrigerate for 20 minutes.

Heat a crepe pan or a small non-stick frying pan over medium heat and lightly grease. Pour in enough batter to coat the base of the pan in a thin, even layer. Tip out any excess. Cook for 1 minute, or until the crepe starts to come away from the side of the pan. Turn over and cook on the other side for a further 1 minute, or until just golden. Repeat the process, stacking the crepes on a plate with greaseproof paper between them and covered with foil, until all the batter is used up.

To serve, put one crepe on a plate. Arrange some raspberries on a quarter of the crepe. Fold the crepe in half, then in half again, so that the raspberries are wrapped in a triangular pocket. Repeat with the remaining crepes and raspberries. Dust with icing sugar and drizzle with maple syrup or honey.

MAKES 8 LARGE CREPES

spiced fruit salad

115 g (4 oz/½ cup) caster (superfine) sugar
4 slices ginger
1 bird's eye chilli, cut in half
juice and zest of 2 limes
fruit, such as a mixture of watermelon, rockmelon, mango, banana,
   cherries, lychees and kiwi fruit — enough for 4 portions

Put the sugar in a saucepan with 125 ml (4 fl oz/½ cup) water and the ginger and chilli. Heat until the sugar melts, then leave to cool before adding the lime juice and zest. Take out the ginger and chilli.

Put your selection of fruit into a bowl and pour over the syrup. Leave to marinate in the fridge for 30 minutes.

SERVES 4

apple and berry crumble muffins

155 g (5½ oz/1¼ cups) self-raising flour
150 g (5½ oz/1 cup) wholemeal self-raising flour
¼ teaspoon ground cinnamon
pinch of ground cloves
115 g (4 oz/½ cup) firmly packed soft brown sugar
185 ml (6 fl oz/¾ cup) milk
2 eggs
125 g (4½ oz) unsalted butter, melted and cooled
2 granny smith apples, peeled, grated
155 g (5½ oz/1 cup) blueberries

CRUMBLE
50 g (1¾ oz) plain (all-purpose) flour
55 g (1¾ oz/¼ cup) demerara sugar
35 g (1¼ oz/⅓ cup) rolled oats
40 g (1½ oz) unsalted butter, chopped

Preheat the oven to 190°C (375°F/Gas 5). Line 12 regular muffin holes with muffin papers. Sift the flours, cinnamon and cloves into a large bowl, add the husks and stir in the sugar. Make a well in the centre.

Put the milk, eggs and butter in a bowl, whisk and pour into the well. Fold until just combined. Fold in the fruit. Divide among the muffin holes.

To make the crumble, put the flour, sugar and oats in a bowl. Rub the butter in with your fingertips until most of the lumps are gone. Sprinkle 2 teaspoons of the crumble over each muffin. Bake for 25 minutes, or until golden. Cool for 5 minutes, then transfer to a wire rack.

MAKES 12 MUFFINS

sweet

apricot and raisin bran loaf

150 g (5½ oz/¾ cup) dried apricots, chopped
160 g (5¾ oz/1 cup) raisins
70 g (2½ oz/1 cup) processed bran cereal
95 g (3¼ oz/½ cup) soft brown sugar
375 ml (13 fl oz/1½ cups) warm milk
125 g (4½ oz/1 cup) self-raising flour, sifted
75 g (2½ oz/½ cup) wholemeal self-raising flour, sifted
1 teaspoon mixed spice

Preheat the oven to 180°C (350°F/Gas 4). Lightly grease a deep 18.5 x 11 cm (7¼ x 4¼ inch) loaf (bar) tin and line the base and sides with baking paper.

Soak the apricots, raisins, bran cereal and brown sugar in the milk in a large bowl for 30 minutes, or until the milk is almost completely absorbed. Stir in the flours and mixed spice to form a stiff moist batter. Spoon the mixture into the tin and smooth the surface.

Bake for 50 minutes, or until a skewer comes out clean when inserted into the centre of the cake — cover with foil during cooking if it browns too much. Leave in the tin for 10 minutes, then turn out onto a wire rack to cool. Cut into thick slices. If desired, serve with butter and dust with icing sugar.

SERVES 6–8

NOTE: Use any dried fruit combination. This loaf is delicious toasted.

sticky gingerbread muffins

250 g (9 oz/2 cups) self-raising flour, sifted
90 g (3¼ oz/¾ cup) plain (all-purpose) flour, sifted
½ teaspoon bicarbonate of soda (baking soda)
3 teaspoons ground ginger
1 teaspoon ground cinnamon
1 teaspoon mixed spice
230 g (8½ oz/1 cup) firmly packed soft brown sugar
55 g (1¾ oz/¼ cup) chopped glacé ginger
235 g (8½ oz/⅔ cup) golden or maple syrup
100 g (3½ oz) unsalted butter, chopped
250 ml (9 fl oz/1 cup) buttermilk
1 egg, lightly beaten

Preheat the oven to 200°C (400°F/Gas 6). Lightly grease 12 regular muffin holes. Put the flours, bicarbonate of soda, ginger, cinnamon and mixed spice in a bowl. Stir in the brown sugar and glacé ginger.

Melt the golden syrup and butter in a saucepan. Cool. Combine the golden or maple syrup mixture, buttermilk and egg and pour into the well. Fold until just combined.

Divide the mixture among the muffin holes. Bake for 20–25 minutes, or until the muffins come away from the side of the tin. Cool for 5 minutes in the tin, then transfer to a wire rack to cool completely.

MAKES 12 MUFFINS

chewy fruit and seed slice

200 g (7 oz) unsalted butter

175 g (6 oz/½ cup) golden or maple syrup

125 g (4½ oz/½ cup) crunchy peanut butter

2 teaspoons natural vanilla extract

30 g (1 oz/¼ cup) plain (all-purpose) flour

30 g (1 oz/⅓ cup) ground almonds

½ teaspoon mixed spice

300 g (10½ oz/3 cups) quick-cooking oats

2 teaspoons finely grated orange zest

185 g (6½ oz/1 cup) soft brown sugar

45 g (1½ oz/½ cup) desiccated coconut

50 g (1¾ oz/⅓ cup) sesame seeds, toasted

90 g (3¼ oz/½ cup) pepitas or shelled sunflower seeds

80 g (2¾ oz/½ cup) raisins, chopped

45 g (1½ oz/¼ cup) mixed peel

Preheat the oven to 170°C (325°F/Gas 3). Lightly grease a 20 x 30 cm (8 x 12 inch) shallow tin and line with baking paper, leaving it hanging over the two long sides.

Place the butter and golden or maple syrup in a small saucepan over low heat, stirring occasionally until melted. Remove from the heat and stir in the peanut butter and vanilla until combined.

Mix together the remaining ingredients, stirring well. Make a well in the centre and add the butter and syrup mixture. Mix with a large metal spoon until combined. Press evenly into the tin and bake for 25 minutes, or until golden and firm. Cool in the tin, then cut into squares.

MAKES 18 PIECES

blueberry muffins

375 g (13 oz/3 cups) plain (all-purpose) flour
1 tablespoon baking powder
165 g (5¾ oz/¾ cup) firmly packed soft brown sugar
125 g (4½ oz) unsalted butter, melted
2 eggs, lightly beaten
250 ml (9 fl oz/1 cup) milk
185 g (6½ oz/1¼ cups) fresh or thawed frozen blueberries

Preheat the oven to 210°C (415°F/Gas 6–7). Lightly grease 12 regular muffin holes. Sift the flour and baking powder into a large bowl. Stir in the sugar and make a well in the centre.

Add the combined melted butter, eggs and milk all at once, and fold until just combined. Do not overmix — the batter should look quite lumpy.

Fold in the blueberries. Spoon the batter into the prepared tin. Bake for 20 minutes, or until golden brown. Cool on a wire rack.

MAKES 12 MUFFINS

sweet

banana and honey loaf

125 g (4½ oz) unsalted butter, softened
140 g (5 oz/¾ cup) soft brown sugar
2 eggs, lightly beaten
2 tablespoons honey
1 large ripe banana, cut into chunks
225 g (8 oz/1½ cups) wholemeal self-raising flour
2 teaspoons ground cinnamon

Preheat the oven to 180°C (350°F/Gas 4). Lightly grease a 22 x 12 cm (8½ x 4½ inch) loaf (bar) tin. Combine the butter and sugar in a food processor for 1 minute, or until lighter in colour. Add the egg and process until combined.

Put 1 tablespoon of the honey in a saucepan over low heat and warm for 1 minute, or until runny. Add to the food processor with the banana and blend until smooth. Add the flour and cinnamon and process until well combined.

Spoon evenly into the tin and bake for 35–40 minutes, or until a skewer comes out clean when inserted into the centre of the loaf. Leave in the tin for 5 minutes before turning out onto a wire rack. Warm the remaining honey in a saucepan over low heat for 1 minute, or until runny. Brush the warm loaf with the warm honey. Serve warm or cool.

SERVES 8

VARIATION: Fold 60 g (2¼ oz/½ cup) chopped walnuts or pecans through the mixture before spooning the mixture into the loaf tin.

red fruit salad with berries

SYRUP
60 g (2¼ oz/¼ cup) caster (superfine) sugar
125 ml (4 fl oz/½ cup) dry red wine
1 star anise
1 teaspoon finely chopped lemon zest

250 g (9 oz/1⅔ cups) strawberries, hulled and halved
150 g (5½ oz/1 cup) blueberries
150 g (5½ oz/1¼ cups) raspberries, mulberries or other red berries
250 g (9 oz) cherries
5 small red plums (about 250 g/9 oz), stones removed and quartered
yoghurt, to serve

To make the syrup, place the sugar, wine, star anise, lemon zest and 125 ml (4 fl oz/½ cup) water in a small saucepan. Bring to the boil over medium heat, stirring to dissolve the sugar. Boil the syrup for 3 minutes, then set aside to cool for 30 minutes. When cool, strain the syrup.

Mix the fruit together in a large bowl and pour on the red wine syrup. Mix well to coat the fruit in the syrup and refrigerate for 1½ hours. Serve the fruit dressed with a little syrup and the yoghurt.

SERVES 6

grilled figs with ricotta

2 tablespoons honey
1 cinnamon stick
3 tablespoons flaked almonds
4 large (or 8 small) figs
125 g (4½ oz/½ cup) ricotta cheese
½ teaspoon natural vanilla extract
2 tablespoons icing (confectioners') sugar, sifted
pinch of ground cinnamon
½ teaspoon finely grated orange zest

Place the honey and cinnamon stick in a small saucepan with 4 tablespoons of water. Bring to the boil, then reduce the heat and simmer gently for 6 minutes, or until thickened and reduced by half. Discard the cinnamon stick and stir in the almonds.

Preheat the grill (broiler) to hot and grease a shallow ovenproof dish large enough to fit all the figs side by side. Slice the figs into quarters from the top to within 1 cm (½ inch) of the bottom, keeping them attached at the base. Arrange in the prepared dish.

Combine the ricotta, vanilla, icing sugar, ground cinnamon and orange zest in a small bowl. Divide the filling among the figs, spooning it into their cavities. Spoon the syrup over the top. Place under the grill and cook until the juices start to come out from the figs and the almonds are lightly toasted. Cool for 2–3 minutes. Spoon the juices and any fallen almonds from the bottom of the dish over the figs and serve.

SERVES 4

index

A

apple and berry crumble muffins 141

apricots

apricot and bran breakfast shake 10, 93

apricot and raisin bran loaf 142

asparagus

potato flowers with salmon, quail eggs and 42

steamed, with crispy pancetta and hard-boiled quail eggs 10

B

bagels with smoked salmon and caper salsa 30

bananas

banana and honey loaf 150

banana, sunflower and pistachio bread 122

creamy rich banana and macadamia smoothie 94

and ripe mango blended with vanilla soy and honey yoghurt 12

with golden syrup and macadamia nuts 8

berry couscous, mixed 105

blt, mediterranean 14

blueberries

blueberry muffins 149

blueberry pancakes 133

bran loaf, apricot and raisin 142

bread, banana, sunflower and pistachio 122

breakfast shake, apricot and bran 10, 93

brioche eggy bread with figs and raspberry cream 126

bruschetta with salmon tartare and roe bubbles 50

C

caffe latte

cardamom, with frangelico 13

decadent, infused with a vanilla bean 12

cappuccino and white-choc muffins 117

capsicum and sweet potato rosti with chipolatas 21

caramelized leek, goat's cheese and spinach tart 38

champagne with strawberries and blackberries 13

cheese and onion waffles with herbed ricotta and roast tomato 61

cheese soufflés, twice-baked 41

chewy fruit and seed slice 146

choc-hazelnut puff pastry rolls 109

cinnamon porridge with caramel figs and cream 102

cinnamon toast, grilled nectarines with 134

citrus compote, minted, with creamed rice 130

classic omelette 82

corn

corn fritters with crispy prosciutto 22

squiggly corn crab cakes 46

couscous, mixed berry 105

crab cakes, squiggly corn 46

creamed rice with minted citrus compote 130

crepes, raspberry breakfast 137

crispy lavash tiles with butter mushrooms 34

crispy prosciutto

corn fritters with 22

french toast with 62

croissants, scrambled eggs and salmon on 57

croque madame 73

D, E

dates, fresh, and sweet figs with honey yoghurt and pine nuts 11

dried fruit slices 11

eggs

eggs benedict 26

fried egg and red onion wrap 78

fried eggs and tomatoes on spring onion potato cakes 65

scrambled, and salmon on brioche 57

scrambled, with cheese and herb cornbread 29
smoky ham, egg and jarlsberg cheese sandwiches 25

F
figs
brioche eggy bread with figs and raspberry cream 126
cinnamon porridge with caramel figs and cream 102
grilled, with ricotta 154
sweet, and fresh dates with honey yoghurt and pine nuts 11
filo sheets, pecan, with fried apples 110
french toast with crispy prosciutto 62
friands, raspberry marshmallow 118
fried eggs
fried egg and red onion wrap 78
tomatoes and, on spring onion potato cakes 65
fried green tomatoes with haloumi 18
fried haloumi, tomato and rocket sandwiches 54
frittatas
mini sweet potato and leek 86
salmon, dill and camembert 17
fritters, corn, with crispy prosciutto 22
fruit platter 10
fruit salad
red, with berries 153
spiced 138
star anise, lime and vanilla tropical 113
fruit, winter, in orange ginger syrup 157

G
ginger ale and fresh pineapple juice punch with ginger, strawberries and mint leaves 12
ginger and ricotta hotcakes with honeycomb 106
ginger tea with lemongrass swizzle sticks 13
gingerbread muffins, sticky 145
goat's cheese
herbed garlic mushrooms with goat's cheese bruschetta 85
spinach tart, caramelized leek and goat's cheese 38
gravlax with parmesan sheets 49
grilled field mushrooms with garlic and chilli 66
grilled figs with ricotta 154
grilled nectarines with cinnamon toast 134

H
haloumi
fried green tomatoes with 18
fried haloumi, tomato and rocket sandwiches 54
ham, egg and jarlsberg cheese sandwiches 25
healthy nut and seed muesli 101
herbed garlic mushrooms with goat's cheese bruschetta 85
high-top cappuccino and white-choc muffins 117

honey yoghurt
fresh banana and ripe mango blended with vanilla soy and 12
sweet figs and fresh dates with, sprinkled with pine nuts 11
hotcakes, ginger and ricotta, with fresh honeycomb 106
huevos rancheros 74

I, K, L
iced chocolate 8
individual herbed lemon ricotta 37

kedgeree 90

lavash tiles, crispy, with butter mushrooms 34
leeks
caramelized leek, goat's cheese and spinach tart 38
mini sweet potato and leek frittatas 86
loaf
apricot and raisin bran loaf 142
banana and honey 150

M
mango, ripe, and fresh banana blended with vanilla soy and honey yoghurt 12
maple yoghurt balls with sugary balsamic pears 98
mediterranean blt 14
mini sweet potato and leek frittatas 86
minted citrus compote with creamed rice 130

mixed berry couscous 105
muesli, healthy nut and
    seed 101
muffins
    apple and berry crumble
        141
    blueberry 149
    passionfruit sugar 125
    sticky gingerbread 145
    white-choc 117
mushrooms
    butter, crispy lavash tiles
        with 34
    grilled field mushrooms
        with garlic and chilli
        66
    herbed garlic
        mushrooms with goat's
        cheese bruschetta 85
    marinated feta with 45
    mushroom omelette
        with chorizo 70
    rocket, mushroom and
        blue cheese omelette
        53

O, P
omelettes
    classic omelette 82
    mushroom omelette
        with chorizo 70
    rocket, mushroom and
        blue cheese 53
    spanish omelette with
        smoked salmon 77

pancakes
    blueberry 133
    rosewater strawberries
        and butter, with 114
pandoro with poached
    peaches and
    mascarpone 97
panettone, toasted, with
    sweet sage, apple and
    cinnamon toddies 8

papaya, red, drizzled with
    tangy lime juice 10
passionfruit sugar muffins
    125
peaches, poached, pandoro
    with mascarpone and
    97
pears, maple yoghurt balls
    with 98
pecan filo sheets with fried
    apples 110
pineapple and starfruit
    slices with maple syrup
    and shaved toasted
    coconut 11
pineapple juice punch and
    ginger ale with ginger,
    strawberries and mint
    leaves 12
piperade 69
poached peaches, pandoro
    with mascarpone and
    97
poached stone fruits 129
pomegranates, red,
    drizzled with rosewater
    and apple juice 11
porridge, cinnamon, with
    caramel figs and cream
    102
potatoes
    potato cakes, spring
        onion, fried eggs and
        tomatoes on 65
    potato flowers with
        salmon, asparagus and
        quail eggs 42
    potato patties, salmon
        and dill, with lime
        mayonnaise 81
    potato tortilla 89
prosciutto, crispy
    corn fritters with 22
    french toast with 62
puff pastry rolls, choc-
    hazelnut 109

Q
quail eggs
    hard-boiled, with
        steamed asparagus and
        crispy pancetta 10
    potato flowers with
        salmon, asparagus and
        42

R
raspberries
    brioche eggy bread with
        figs and raspberry
        cream 126
    raspberry breakfast
        crepes 137
    raspberry marshmallow
        friands 118
red fruit salad with berries
    153
rhubarb with vanilla
    and cardamom rice
    121
rice
    creamed, with minted
        citrus compote 130
    vanilla and cardamom,
        with rhubarb 121
ricotta, individual herbed
    lemon 37
rocket
    fried haloumi, tomato
        and rocket sandwiches
        54
    rocket, mushroom and
        blue cheese omelette
        53
rosti, sweet potato and
    capsicum, with
    chipolatas 21

S
salmon
    bagels with smoked
        salmon and caper
        salsa 30

bruschetta with salmon tartare and roe bubbles 50

gravlax with parmesan sheets 49

potato flowers with asparagus, quail eggs and 42

salmon and dill potato patties with lime mayonnaise 81

salmon, dill and camembert frittata 17

scrambled eggs and salmon on brioche 57

spanish omelette with smoked salmon 77

sandwiches

fried haloumi, tomato and rocket sandwiches 54

smoky ham, egg and jarlsberg cheese 25

savoury breakfast tarts 58

scrambled eggs

cheese and herb cornbread, with 29

salmon on brioche and 57

sheep's milk yoghurt with puréed strawberries 9

slice, chewy fruit and seed 146

smoked salmon

caper salsa bagels and 30

spanish omelette with 77

smoky ham, egg and jarlsberg cheese sandwiches 25

smoothie, creamy rich banana and macadamia 94

spanish omelette with smoked salmon 77

spiced fruit salad 138

spinach tart, caramelized leek and goat's cheese 38

spring onion potato cakes, fried eggs and tomatoes on 65

squiggly corn crab cakes 46

star anise, lime and vanilla tropical fruit salad 113

starfruit and pineapple slices with maple syrup and shaved toasted coconut 11

sticky gingerbread muffins 145

stone fruits, poached 129

strawberries

champagne with strawberries and blackberries 13

pancakes with rosewater strawberries and butter 114

sugar bananas, halved, with golden syrup and macadamia nuts 8

sweet figs and fresh dates with honey yoghurt sprinkled with pine nuts 11

sweet potato

mini sweet potato and leek frittatas 86

sweet potato and capsicum rosti with chipolatas 21

T

tarts

savoury breakfast 58

spinach, caramelized leek and goat's cheese 38

tea, ginger, with lemongrass swizzle sticks 13

toasted pannetone with sweet sage, apple and cinnamon toddies 8

tomatoes

cheese and onion waffles with herbed ricotta and roast tomato 61

fried eggs and tomatoes on spring onion potato cakes 65

fried green, with haloumi 18

fried haloumi, tomato and rocket sandwiches 54

tortilla, potato 89

tropical fruit salad, star anise, lime and vanilla 113

twice-baked cheese soufflés 41

V, W

vodka, tomato juice, tabasco, worcestershire and celery salt 13

waffles, cheese and onion, with herbed ricotta and roast tomato 61

watermelon and honeydew rock melon on skewers 9

white-choc muffins 117

whitebait with crème fraîche tartare 33

wrap, fried egg and red onion 78

Y

yoghurt

maple yoghurt balls with sugary balsamic pears 98

sheep's milk, with puréed strawberries 9

Published in 2007 by Murdoch Books Pty Limited
www.murdochbooks.com.au

Murdoch Books Australia
Pier 8/9
23 Hickson Road
Millers Point NSW 2000
Phone: +61 (0) 2 8220 2000
Fax: +61 (0) 2 8220 2558

Murdoch Books UK Limited
Erico House
6th Floor
93–99 Upper Richmond Road
Putney, London SW15 2TG
Phone: +44 (0) 20 8785 5995
Fax: +44 (0) 20 8785 5985

Chief Executive: Juliet Rogers
Publishing Director: Kay Scarlett

Design manager: Vivien Valk
Project manager: Janine Flew
Editor: Gordana Trifunovic
Design concept: Alex Frampton
Designer: Susanne Geppert
Production: Maiya Levitch
Photography: Tanya Zouev, Chris Chen, Ben Dearnley
Styling: Katy Holder, Kristen Anderson, Michelle Noerianto, Suzie Smith
Food preparation: Ross Dobson, Angela Tregonning, Michaela le Compte, Valli Little,
Tracey Meharg, Jody Vassallo
Cover photography: Petrina Tinslay
Recipes by Jody Vassallo

National Library of Australia Cataloguing-in-Publication Data
Marie Claire breakfast. Includes index.
ISBN 9781740459587. ISBN 1 74045 958 X.
1. Breakfasts. 641.52

Printed by Midas Printing (Asia) Ltd in 2007. PRINTED IN CHINA.

IMPORTANT: Those who might be at risk from the effects of salmonella poisoning (the elderly,
pregnant women, young children and those suffering from immune deficiency diseases) should
consult their doctor with any concerns about eating raw eggs.

CONVERSION GUIDE: You may find cooking times vary depending on the oven you are using.
For fan-forced ovens, as a general rule, set the oven temperature to 20°C (35°F) lower than
indicated in the recipe. We have used 20 ml (4 teaspoon) tablespoon measures. If you are using
a 15 ml (3 teaspoon) tablespoon, for most recipes the difference will not be noticeable. However,
for recipes using baking powder, gelatine, bicarbonate of soda (baking soda), small amounts of
flour and cornflour (cornstarch), add an extra teaspoon for each tablespoon specified.